Also by Danielle S. LeBlanc:

Recipes for Unusual Gluten Free Pasta: Pierogis, Dumplings, Desserts and More!

Living with Oral Allergy Syndrome: A Gluten and Meat-Free Cookbook for Soy, Wheat, Fresh Fruit and Vegetable Allergies

Danielle S. LeBlanc

La Venta West, Inc
Vancouver, Canada

La Venta West Inc.
Vancouver, Canada

Copyright © 2014 Danielle S. LeBlanc
Photographs copyright © 2014 Danielle S. LeBlanc
Cover design by cooking@fiverr.com

All rights reserved. No part of this book may be reproduced or utilized in any form or by any means, electronic or mechanical, including photocopying, recording, or by any information storage and retrieval system, without permission in writing from the publisher.

This book is intended as an informational guide. The recipes and techniques described herein are for educational purposes only, and not meant as a substitute for professional medical care or treatment. Please read the suggested contents of each recipe carefully and determine whether or not they may create a problem for you. We are not responsible for any hazards, loss or damage that may occur as a result of any recipe use or use of information provided herein. In the event of any doubt, please contact your medical advisor prior to use.

ISBN (eBook) 978-0-9920802-9-7
ISBN (paperback) 978-0-9920802-8-0

DEDICATION

To Alex, resident beer drinker.

CONTENTS

Dedication, 5

Foreword by Brian Kolodzinski, 9

Introduction, 11

Chapter 1: Tips & Tricks for Cooking & Baking with Gluten Free Beer, 13

Chapter 2: Boozy Breakfasts & Baked Goods, 17

Chapter 3: Bibacious Mains, 33

Chapter 4: Capernoited Condiments, Soups, and Sides, 47

Chapter 5: Dionysian Desserts, 63

FOREWORD
BY BRIAN KOLODZINSKI

A gluten free diet is a culinary journey that many people will never have the privilege of enjoying. It allows us to defy convention and embrace change while overcoming the various reasons that lead us to a gluten free diet. We dabble in culinary traditions that represent other people and their cultures to create wonderful meals. The infusion of traditional and new ingredients creates new meals that are enjoyed and heal our bodies.

Gluten free beer has traveled along the same winding path as gluten free food. For many years gluten free food was uniquely different than traditional foods. Gluten free beer was also uniquely different than traditional beers. But just as gluten free foods have become as enjoyable as tradition foods, so have gluten free beers. And nowhere is that more true than when you brew your own craft gluten free beer at home.

My adventures in brewing gluten free beer are greatly influenced by my passion for beer. I was born and raised in Milwaukee, Wisconsin where beer is a large part of the local culture. I moved to the Pacific Northwest where microbreweries enhanced my palate for great beer. It was difficult to limit myself to the few gluten free beers available on the market. And thus began my endeavor in brewing beer at home.

Over the years I have had the privilege of working with malters and master brewers from around the world. This has allowed Gluten Free Home Brewing LLC to foster partnerships and friendships with the pioneers of gluten free beer brewing in the United States. In addition to tutorials and a recipe database, Gluten Free Home Brewing LLC offers a dedicated gluten free facility that provides the largest selection of gluten free brewing ingredients and supplies.

While researching gluten free beer recipes, I discovered that the oldest known written recipe in the world is a 4,000 year old recipe for beer. Centuries later we now share great recipes all around the world. Poor and Gluten Free blogger Danielle S. LeBlanc's newest book, *Cooking And Baking With Gluten Free Beer*, brings together her great knowledge of gluten free recipes with an ingredient we all love, beer! Danielle and I both embarked on our gluten free journeys for health reasons. Danielle began a blog about food while I began a blog about beer. We have amassed a wealth of knowledge from personal experiences and newly acquired expertise.

Cooks, bakers and brewers will all enjoy the culinary delights found within this new book. Beer adds unique and complex flavors that enhance traditional dishes. The various styles of beer means you can incorporate the characteristics you enjoy about your favorite beers with dishes you have enjoyed for years. And of course many of the recipes contained in this book can be enjoyed along with drinking a beer.

Whether or not you intend on brewing your own beer, you will still enjoy the wide variety of recipes brought together in this collection. One of my first cookbooks as a young culinary enthusiast was about cooking with beer. I again look forward to sampling the culinary delights in Danielle's book, served with a craft gluten free beer made in my home.

Brian Kolodzinski

www.glutenfreehomebrewing.org
The Only Homebrew Store Dedicated
to Your Gluten Free Brewing Needs

INTRODUCTION

Why waste that rare and precious gluten free beer on cooking and baked goods?

Well, beer is a particularly useful addition to gluten free foods. Beer serves as a leavening agent in those GF baked goods that tend to be heavy, dense, and chewy. The carbon dioxide in beer helps baked goods rise, and lends a lighter, flakier texture to buns, breads, and rolls. Beer also tenderizes meat, while lending a deeper flavor to vegan sauces, chili, and gravy. In dessert, beer enriches the deep dark chocolate essence, balancing it with the slightly bitter taste of hops.

Practical reasons aside, there's also something deeply satisfying and entertaining about biting into a dish made with a bottle of one of your favorite beers. It's pleasurable to taste the rich, boozy undertones discernible in a stout pot pie, drunken meatballs, or a yeasty lager bread.

And boy are these are exciting times for gluten free beer drinkers...

The joys of cooking and baking with beer have long been denied those of us with gluten issues. Back in 2009, when I first discovered I was gluten intolerant, there were very few decent GF beers on the market, and those that existed were expensive and hard to find. Now, however, more and more breweries are recognizing the demand for good gluten free beer. We want more than GF beer that tastes like cider steeped in soggy cardboard with a "Pale Ale" labelled slapped on it. We want pale ales and stouts and IPAs and pilsners. *We want gluten free beer that tastes like real beer.*

Breweries and brew supply shops are rising to meet the demand. Some breweries are exclusively dedicated to GF beer, while established breweries are now making beer with all gluten free ingredients. These brews make use of GF grains like sorghum, rice, millet, corn, and buckwheat, rather than the traditional wheat and barley. Still others are finding ways to strip the gluten from their old recipes to create beer that comes in under the minimum amount of gluten required to be labelled as gluten free. It's even possible, although not always easy, to find organic, gluten free beer.

Things are looking up for those of us who like to drink beer, sans gluten of course. There's still a long ways to go, but it is becoming more commonplace to walk into a liquor store and have more than one GF beer to choose from. Some enlightened pubs even have GF beer on tap. *On tap,* people! Furthermore, people like Brian Kolodzinski of *Gluten Free Home Brewing.com* are experimenting with brewing their own GF beer, brewing beer at home that is just as good, if not better, than some of the best craft beers.

So now that we're finally able to kick back with a six pack of cold gluten free beer on a Sunday afternoon, like all the normal glutinous folks can do, why shouldn't we also be able to enjoy all the other wonderful things that can be made with beer?

My husband and I spent three years living in Madison, Wisconsin, where beer - and subsequently pub food made with beer - is practically a gastronomic science. This book came into being because my husband, who doesn't actually have any issues with gluten, happens to really enjoy beer and food made with it. During our time in Wisconsin we ate at a lot of pubs. My husband sampled - and since I'm gluten intolerant, I sniffed and poked at - quite a lot of booze-infused dishes. I wanted to try and recreate the pub food he loves, along with a variety of things we hadn't found in local restaurants. But in order to sample the food I was cooking and baking, I had to make it gluten free. As with all my other cookbooks, my husband Alex has been my #1 tester, although perhaps with this one he's been a little more enthusiastically so.

So in this little book, you'll find what you need to enjoy beer around the clock, from breakfast through to dessert. Relax on Sunday morning with *Fuddled French Toast, Bacchic Biscuits,* or *Scuppered Sweet Potato Crepes*. Then try a lunch of *Deconstructed Sorghum & Citrus Salad* with *Muddled Meatballs* and *Rip-Roaring Rosemary Bread* on the side. Move on to a booze-infused dinner, starting with *Brewski Stew,* stumbling through to *Tie-One-On Fish Tacos* with a side of *Merry, Moon-Eyed Mussels* and ending with *Borracho Mexican Chocolate Cupcakes with Kahlua Frosting.*

In the next chapter you'll also find tips and tricks for cooking and baking with gluten free beer that will help guide you in your own experimentation with GF beer. Beer is a wonderful addition to GF foods, and once you get the hang of it, you'll want to try it in everything!

***

Many of the recipes in this book also have vegetarian and vegan alternatives, because non-meat eaters deserve to enjoy beer, too! **Recipes with vegan options are marked with a (V), and have been tested to ensure the vegan substitutes work.** Those without a (V) may still be vegetarian, dairy-free, or pescatarian, but not vegan. Other recipes may also work with vegan substitutes, but haven't been tested to ensure texture or taste.

CHAPTER 1:
TIPS & TRICKS
FOR COOKING & BAKING WITH GLUTEN FREE BEER

As mentioned earlier, beer is an excellent addition to gluten free cooking and baking. However, there are a few things to keep in mind when using the recipes in this book, or for experimenting on your own. The range of available GF beers in not nearly as wide as regular beers, nor are certain beers as widely available as others. This makes it harder to provide specific recommendations for the type of beer to use in each recipe. The below suggestions are to help guide you when choosing beer for use in certain recipes, as well as suggestions for trying out your own recipes and ideas.

1) **Ensure that the beer you are using is, in fact, gluten free and safe *for you*.** I stress this because there is a wider variety of GF beer on the market now than ever before. Some products are made with completely gluten free ingredients, such as sorghum, millet, rice, and corn, while others have been made with glutinous grains, such as barley and wheat, but have had the gluten stripped out.

Some countries allow products to be labelled as "gluten free" if they contain less than 20 ppm (parts per million) gluten. This is considered by many health authorities to be a safe level of gluten even for those with celiac disease. GF beers that are made with barley or wheat have had the gluten stripped out during processing, and must contain less than 20 ppm gluten in order to be labelled as GF, depending on which country they're sold in.

However, the safety of these beers and other GF products with low-gluten content has been an ongoing debate within the gluten free community. While some people might be ok with GF beers that are made with glutinous ingredients, others have reported reactions to some of these low-gluten beers. This may depend on your personal level of sensitivity and comfort.

Furthermore, buckwheat, millet, sorghum, rice, corn, hops, and yeast are common ingredients in GF beer. If you have allergies to any of these or any other ingredients in your GF beer of choice, you'll want to proceed with caution to avoid any adverse reactions.

2) **Don't cook or bake with beer you wouldn't drink.** If it tastes terrible on its own, it probably won't make your recipe any better.

3) **The longer beer is cooked, the more bitter it becomes.** Hops give beer its bitter flavor. The longer beer (and therefore hops) is cooked, the more bitter the hops will get. Hoppy beers,

such as India Pale Ales (IPA), will quickly become bitter and overpower most stews, gravies, and sauces.

4) **Add beer towards the end in stews and sauces.** This will prevent the bitterness mentioned above, and will also prevent the loss of the delicate aroma of hops.

5) **Add something sweet, such as pureed carrots, sweet potatoes, or lemon juice to stews that have become bitter.** Balancing overcooked hops with something sweet, or something that will cut the bitterness, can help rectify a recipe gone wrong.

6) **Other sweeteners that balance bitter beer and enhance malt flavors include rice syrup, molasses, maple syrup, or sorghum syrup.**

7) **Pale ales (except IPAs) tend to be the most versatile for baking.** Their light citrus and floral tones blend particularly well in baked goods.

8) **Lagers, stouts, and porters often go well with chocolate, meat, stews, and recipes that call for a stronger, richer flavor.**

9) **In general, IPAs are not great for cooking with**. They are very hoppy (see above notes) and bitterness increases with cooking time.

10) **Beer is excellent in stews** as a replacement for stock or wine. It adds a full-bodied flavor. Add beer towards the end to prevent bitterness.

11) **The carbonation in beer allows the batter in fried foods to brown faster and better.** It also creates a lighter, airier batter.

12) **Beer is an excellent marinade for meat.** It tenderizes meat, like chicken, steak, and pork, and provides a juicy glaze. Meat can be marinated in beer (mixed with salt, garlic, or onions) for about 24 hours, then discard the beer and cook as desired.

13) **Shellfish, like mussels and clams, are wonderful steamed in beer**. The beer lends seafood a subtle flavor, and bread can be dipped into the beer broth afterwards.

14) **Not all alcohol evaporates during cooking and baking.** A study by the U.S. Department of Agriculture found that even after 25 minutes of baking, 40% of alcohol remained in alcoholic beverages.[1] The amount of beer in most recipes is small, and the average portion is not enough to affect anyone, but it's worth keeping in mind that not *all* the alcohol is cooked or boiled away.

---

[1] USDA Table of Nutrient Retention Factors, Release 6 (report), U.S. Department of Agriculture, 2007, page 12. http://www.ars.usda.gov/SP2UserFiles/Place/80400525/Data/retn/retn06.pdf

15) **Cold beer mixed with cold, high fat milk / cream is less likely to curdle.** Mixing beer and milk can cause milk to curdle, leaving recipes with a grainy texture. The higher the fat content of the milk or cream (such as whipping cream), and the colder and fresher both the milk and beer are, the less likely it is to curdle. Mix together slowly.

16) **Don't forget the foam factor**. Beer foams when added to other ingredients, so make sure your bowls and pots are large enough to account for a mild volcanic explosion.

17) **Vegan beer?** Most beer is made with vegan ingredients such as sorghum, rice, millet, corn, and buckwheat. However, in some cases there is a small chance that animal products were somehow used in the process of brewing. If this is a concern, check with the particular brewery you are interested in before using the beer.

18) **Don't waste that beer!** Some of the recipes in this book only call for a smaller amount of beer vs. a full beer. Why not plan a meal around using one beer, for example, and make *Fubared Flatbread* to serve with an *On-a-Bender Burger*? Or make *Fuddled French Toast* for breakfast one day, refrigerate the remaining beer and use it the next day in *Tanked-Up Tofu Balls*. Of course, you could always just drink what's left!

Beer with breakfast? Why not? Beer helps make baked goods light and fluffy. Pale ales and other beers with fruity or citrus tones lend tenderness to biscuits, scones, pizza dough, and other doughy goods. So now tell me if there's any good reason not to have beer with breakfast!

Shown below: Bacchic Biscuits

Chapter 2:
BOOZY BREAKFASTS & BAKED GOODS

Blitzed Blueberry Scones

IN THIS CHAPTER:

Blitzed Blueberry Scones (V)

Fuddled French Toast

Fubared Flatbread (V)

Bacchic Biscuits (V)

Scuppered Sweet Potato Crepes (V)

Raddled Cinnamon Rolls (V)

Cockeyed Salsa Cornbread (V)

Pixilated Pretzel Bites (V)

Rip-Roaring Rosemary Bread

BLITZED BLUEBERRY SCONES (V)

Flaky, lemony, and light, these scones also freeze well and can be reheated in the microwave for 30-40 seconds for breakfast or brunch on those "morning-after" mornings.

Makes 8 large or 16 small scones

1 cup sorghum flour
½ cup millet flour (or white rice flour or more sorghum)
½ cup tapioca starch + extra for dusting
½ tsp salt
½ Tbsp baking powder
¼ tsp baking soda
½ tsp xanthan gum
1 tsp lemon zest
8 Tbsp chilled butter, cut into chunks (or dairy-free substitute)
1 egg (or 1 Tbsp flax meal mixed with 2 Tbsp hot water)
½ cup cold GF beer
⅓ cup blueberries

<u>Frosting</u>
1 Tbsp lemon juice
½ cup icing sugar

Preheat oven to 400F and line a baking sheet with parchment paper.

1. In the bowl of a food processor or large bowl, sift the flours, starch, salt, baking powder, soda, and xanthan gum. Pulse in the lemon zest and butter until crumbly, or cut in zest and butter with a pastry cutter or two knives. Mix in egg and beer until just combined. Do not over mix. Fold in blueberries.

2. Lightly flour a flat surface with tapioca starch. Turn out dough and shape it into a round about ¾" high and 7" in diameter. Or, for smaller scones, divide dough in half and shape two rounds ¾" high by 3.5-4" in diameter. Cut diagonally across the circle to create 8 triangles.

3. Arrange scones on baking sheet so they do not touch. Bake for 15-17 minutes, until lightly browned on top, and cool on a rack.

4. Mix together frosting ingredients and drizzle over cooled scones.

FUDDLED FRENCH TOAST

A great Sunday morning breakfast, this French toast needs little introduction. A pale ale or lager would work well along with a soft white bread, such as the *Rip-Roaring Rosemary Bread* in this chapter.

Serves 6

2/3 cup cold GF beer
½ cup cold milk
2 Tbsp sugar
2 eggs, beaten
1 tsp vanilla
½ tsp cinnamon
2 Tbsp butter + more as needed
1 loaf soft GF bread, sliced

1. Beat beer, milk, sugar, eggs, vanilla, and cinnamon together.

2. Heat a skillet over medium heat. Melt butter in skillet. Dip bread slices in beer batter and arrange in skillet. Cook 3-4 minutes on one side, until golden brown. Flip and cook until both sides are browned. Repeat with remaining bread slices.

Serve with maple syrup, honey, jam, or icing sugar sprinkled on top.

FUBARED FLATBREAD (V)

A quick and easy flatbread that can be made start to finish in under 30 minutes. It's a great sandwich bread, and perfect for dipping in *Sotted Chocolate Chili* or *Bollixed Black Bean Soup*. It freezes well and can be reheated in the oven or microwave.

Makes 1 thick or 2 thin 9 x 13" flatbreads

1 cup sorghum flour
½ cup tapioca starch
1 Tbsp honey or sugar
½ tsp baking soda
½ Tbsp baking powder
1 tsp xanthan gum
½ tsp salt + more for sprinkling
½ cup GF beer (pale ale or lager)
¼ cup + 2 Tbsp water
2 Tbsp vegetable oil or olive oil
2 eggs (or 2 Tbsp flax meal mixed with 6 Tbsp warm water)
Optional: ½ Tbsp dried onion flakes, ¼ tsp garlic powder, ½ Tbsp dried rosemary, ½ cup shredded cheddar cheese, chopped olives

Preheat oven to 350F. Spray 1 or 2 baking sheets with oil and cover with parchment paper.

1. Sift dry ingredients in a medium-sized bowl, adding in optional ingredients.

2. In a large bowl, whisk together beer, water, oil, and eggs. Add in dry ingredients and mix until a smooth paste is formed. This will be sticky.

3. If making 2 flatbreads, divide dough. Spread over baking sheets with a wet spatula and sprinkle with extra salt.

4. Bake 13-15 minutes, until lightly browned and springy to the touch. Remove from oven and cool.

BACCHIC BISCUITS (V)

The ability of beer to lighten baked goods is particularly apparent in these biscuits, making them light and fluffy. They also freeze well, and can be reheated in the microwave for 30-40 seconds, or in the oven.

Makes approximately 12 biscuits

1 ¼ cup sorghum flour or brown rice flour
¾ cup tapioca starch + extra for dusting
1 tsp xanthan gum
1 Tbsp + 1 tsp baking powder
¾ tsp baking soda
¾ tsp salt
1 Tbsp sugar

¼ cup butter (or dairy-free substitute)
1 egg (or 1 Tbsp ground flax mixed with 3 Tbsp warm water)
½ cup GF beer at room temp (such as pale ale)
¼ cup milk of choice (regular, almond, rice milk, etc.), at room temp
Optional: 1 cup shredded sharp cheddar cheese, divided

Preheat oven to 400F and line a baking sheet with parchment paper.

1. In a bowl or in a food processor, sift dry ingredients. Cut in butter with a pastry cutter, or pulse in blender just until crumbly.
2. Whisk egg into milk and beer. Fold liquid gently into the dry ingredients, adding in ¾ cup optional cheese. Do not over-blend.
3. Cover a flat surface with waxed paper and dust with tapioca starch. Dust hands with starch and pat dough into a circle approximately 7-8" in diameter.
4. Dip a biscuit cutter approximately 3" in diameter (or the rim of a glass), into the tapioca starch. Cut out biscuit shapes and arrange on baking sheet so they do not touch. Combine scraps and shape more biscuits until dough is finished. Sprinkle with remaining cheddar cheese if desired.
5. Bake 15 minutes. Remove to a cooling rack.

Breakfasts & Baked Goods

SCUPPERED SWEET POTATO CREPES (V)

Golden orange, these crepes are flexible and naturally sweet. Serve plain, sprinkled with icing sugar, or with fruit fillings. Or serve as dessert with whipped cream or *Peely-Wally Pudding*, as shown above.

Makes 8 – 6" crepes

½ cup GF beer (such as pale ale or lager)
½ cup milk (cow, almond, or rice)
1 egg (or 1 Tbsp flax meal mixed with 3 Tbsp water)
½ cup sweet potato
½ tsp vanilla
½ cup sorghum flour
¼ cup tapioca starch
½ Tbsp sugar
¼ tsp salt
½ tsp cinnamon
⅛ tsp ginger
⅛ tsp nutmeg
Butter or oil for frying

1. Whisk together beer, milk, and egg until frothy. Mix in sweet potato and vanilla until smooth.

2. Sift together sorghum, tapioca, sugar, salt, cinnamon, ginger, and nutmeg. Fold in to the beer mix and mix until smooth.

3. Heat a small skillet over medium heat. Grease with 1 Tbsp butter or oil. Spread approximately ¼ cup batter in skillet. Cover with a lid and cook 2-3 minutes. Remove cover and cook 1 minute, until edges begin to appear dry. Flip and cook another 2-3 minutes, until both sides are golden brown.

Remove from heat and repeat with remaining batter until finished.

Breakfasts & Baked Goods

RADDLED CINNAMON ROLLS (V)

Fluffy and only slightly sweet, these cinnamon rolls can be served any time of day. They're best served warm to keep them soft, and can be reheated for 15 seconds in the microwave or popped in the oven for a minute or two. They also freeze well.

Makes 15 rolls

1 tsp cinnamon
1½ Tbsp sugar
½ cup warm water
1 Tbsp yeast
1 tsp sugar
1 cup tapioca starch
1½ cup sorghum flour
1 Tbsp baking powder
1 tsp salt
2 tsp xanthan gum
2 Tbsp sugar

Rice flour for dusting
½ cup GF beer (pale ale or lager)
1/4 cup milk (cow, rice, almond, or soy)
1/4 cup olive or coconut oil
2 Tbsp melted butter or dairy free alternative

For Frosting
¾ cup powdered sugar
1 Tbsp + 1 tsp beer
¼ teaspoon vanilla

Grease a baking sheet and/or line with parchment paper.

1. Mix together the 1 tsp cinnamon and 1½ Tbsp sugar. Set aside.

2. Mix the water, yeast, and sugar together. Set aside and let rise no longer than 5-7 minutes.

3. In a large bowl, sift all the dry ingredients together, except extra rice flour for dusting. Add in the beer, milk, oil, and yeast mixture and blend until smooth. The mix will be quite wet.

4. **To roll out the dough**: Lay out a large piece of plastic wrap or waxed paper, tape it to the counter, and dust with rice flour. Turn out the dough, sprinkle with more flour, and cover with another sheet of plastic wrap or waxed paper. Roll out dough into a long rectangle with a rolling pin, about ¼" thick. Remove top sheet. Brush with ½ the melted butter and sprinkle with cinnamon sugar mix.

To make rolls: Lift the edge of the bottom layer of plastic, using plastic to lift the dough up and over, peeling back the plastic as you go to create a roll. Slice roll into rounds about 1" thick with a sharp knife. A wet knife works best - moisten every couple of slices. Gently place on baking sheet, allowing space for rolls to rise and spread. Brush with more melted butter.

5. Allow the rolls to rise in a warm place for 30 minutes. Bake in 375F oven 15 minutes, until slightly browned and spongy. Remove from heat and cool on a rack.

To make frosting: Whisk together all ingredients for frosting in a bowl. Drizzle glaze on cinnamon rolls.

For best texture, serve warm.

Breakfasts & Baked Goods

COCKEYED SALSA CORNBREAD (V)

This cornmeal bread has a deep, complex flavor thanks to the combo of salsa and beer. Serve it with a healthy topping of honey, cheese, sorghum syrup, or crumble it into *Sotted Chocolate Chili* with a beer on the side for a well-balanced meal! The bread can be sliced and frozen, then reheated later in the microwave for 35-40 seconds.

Makes one 8" square dish or 8" cast iron skillet

1 cup cornmeal
½ cup sorghum flour
½ cup tapioca starch
1 Tbsp baking powder
1 tsp salt
½ tsp baking soda
⅓ cup brown sugar
¾ cup GF beer (pale ale or lager)
¼ cup prepared salsa
2 Tbsp olive oil
½ cup applesauce (or vegetable oil or soft butter)
2 eggs (or 2 Tbsp ground flaxseed mixed with 6 Tbsp water)
Oil or melted butter for greasing

Preheat oven to 375F. Grease an 8x8" baking dish or an 8" cast iron skillet.

1. Mix cornmeal, sorghum, tapioca, baking powder, salt, baking soda, and sugar together.

2. Mix wet ingredients together. Add dry to wet and beat until smooth. Pour into greased dish and bake 20-25 minutes, until top is golden brown and a toothpick inserted in the centre comes out clean. Remove from oven and cool in the dish 15 minutes to set. Best served warm.

Breakfasts & Baked Goods

PIXILATED PRETZEL BITES (V)

Crispy on the outside and soft on the inside, these pretzel bites are perfect for game days. Especially when served with *Disorderly Cheddar Dip*. These are best served warm and within 24 hours.

Makes about 60 pieces

½ cup GF beer (lager or pale ale)
1 ½ Tbsp sugar
1 package active dry yeast
1 cup sorghum flour
⅓ cup tapioca starch
2 Tbsp sweet rice flour + extra for dusting
1 tsp xanthan gum
½ tsp salt
1 egg, beaten (or 1 Tbsp flax meal mixed with 3 Tbsp water)
Oil (such as olive, coconut, or vegetable oil)
2 Tbsp melted butter (or dairy-free substitute)
Coarse sea salt

For soda bath
6 cups water
2 Tbsp baking soda
1 tsp salt

Grease a large bowl with oil.

1. Warm beer to 110F in a pot or microwave. In a large bowl, mix together beer, sugar, and yeast. Set aside and let rise 7 minutes.

2. Sift together sorghum, tapioca, sweet rice flour, xanthan, and salt. Add ½ flour mix to beer mix, along with the egg. Mix well until blended, then add remaining flour mix and beat until smooth. Dough will be quite goopy. Form dough into a ball shape and turn into greased bowl. Brush dough with oil. Set aside in a warm place and let rise 30-45 minutes, until almost doubled.

3. Dust a flat surface with sweet rice flour. Divide dough into eight pieces. Roll out pieces into ropes 1" thick. With a wet knife, cut into 1" pieces.

4. Preheat oven to 375F and cover two baking sheets with parchment paper. Prepare the soda bath by mixing together water, soda, and salt in a large pot. Bring soda bath to a boil. Drop in pretzel bites and boil until they float, about 25 seconds. Drain with a slotted spoon and remove to baking sheets. Be careful not to over boil.

5. Brush bites with melted butter and sprinkle with sea salt. Bake until light brown, 10-15 minutes. Remove from heat and serve with dipping sauce, such as *Disorderly Cheddar Dip*.

Pretzel bites are best served warm, and within 24 hours.

Breakfasts & Baked Goods

RIP-ROARING ROSEMARY BREAD

Soft yet sturdy, this bread makes great sandwiches. Or slice it up for *Fuddled French Toast*, or for scooping up *Sotted Chocolate Chili*. It is savory, and the flavor can be amped up by using a stronger beer, such as a lager, or tone it down with a pale ale. It can be sliced and frozen for use later. Remove from the microwave and let defrost, or defrost individual slices in the microwave for 20 seconds, or in the toaster.

Makes 1- 9" loaf

1 packet active dry yeast
1 ½ cups GF beer, heated to 110F
1 tsp sugar
1 cup sorghum flour
1 cup white rice flour
1 cup tapioca flour
1 ½ tsp xanthan gum
1 ½ Tbsp baking powder
1 ½ tsp salt
¼ cup sugar
1 Tbsp dried rosemary
2 eggs, beaten and at room temp
2 Tbsp unsalted butter + extra for greasing (or 1 Tbsp olive oil)
Optional: ½ cup shredded cheddar

Preheat oven to 375F. Grease a 9" loaf pan with butter or oil.

1. In a small bowl, combine yeast, beer, and sugar. Set aside and let rise 7 minutes.

2. Sift sorghum, rice flour, tapioca, xanthan gum, baking powder, salt, sugar, and rosemary together in a large bowl. Add in optional cheese or rosemary and blend. Mix in eggs and yeast mixture until smooth. Batter will be goopy. Scoop into greased loaf pan and smooth top over. Drizzle with melted butter, or brush with olive oil.

3. Bake 40-50 minutes, until risen and top is golden brown. Top will be cracked open. Remove from oven and turn out onto a cooling rack. Cool 15 minutes to set before cutting.

Beer lends a depth of flavor to a variety of conventional, and not-so-conventional main dishes, whether they are meat-based or layered with sauerkraut. Whether it be lunch or dinner, pub fare or an upscale entrée, there's a little something for everyone here.

Shown below: Boozy Beer Brined Chicken

Chapter 3:
BIBACIOUS MAINS

Plotzed Poor Man's Pierogi

IN THIS CHAPTER:

Plotzed Poor Man's Pierogi (V)

Tipsy Pot Pie (V)

Sotted Chocolate Chili (V)

Boozy Beer Brined Chicken

Been-at-Barbados Battered Fish

Tie-One-On Fish Tacos

Blotto Brats and Kraut

Pie-Eyed Pizza Dough (V)

Hop-Headed Ham

On-a-Bender Burger

Merry Moon-Eyed Mussels

PLOTZED POOR MAN'S PIEROGI (V)

Polish pierogi are often served stuffed with sauerkraut and topped with sour cream. This dish does away with the labor-intensive pierogi wrapping and is cooked with noodles instead. It is often known as Poor Man's Piergoi, or Lazy Pierogi because it's quick and easy to make.

Serves 4-6

1 ½ Tbsp butter (or dairy-free substitute)
½ onion, minced
1 – 32 oz jar sauerkraut, drained
2 tart apples, peeled and diced (or ½ cup applesauce)
1 cup GF pale ale, or other citrus-toned beer
¼ tsp black pepper
½ Tbsp brown sugar
8 oz dry GF spiral noodles, cooked
Salt and pepper to taste
Optional: cooked bacon, sausage, parmesan cheese, or 2 oz canned sliced mushrooms

1. In a large pot, heat butter over medium heat. Add minced onion and sauté 5-7 minutes to soften.

2. Turn heat up to medium-high, add sauerkraut, apples, pale ale, and pepper and cook until liquid is almost all gone. Mix in brown sugar, cooked noodles, and optional ingredients. Cook just until all ingredients are heated through, remove from heat and serve.

TIPSY POT PIE (V)

Vegan or not, this pot pie is hearty and filling with a buttery, flaky crust. It's even better reheated the next day when the flavors have had time to blend.

Makes 1 – 9" pie plate

1 lb boneless, skinless chicken breasts, cubed
(for a vegan option, eliminate chicken and add 1 cup soft veggies, such as broccoli, zucchini, or corn in the last 5 minutes of boiling the harder vegetables)
1 cup finely diced carrots
¾ cup finely diced russet potatoes
¾ cup shelled green peas
2 cup GF stock
2 Tbsp olive oil or butter
⅓ cup finely diced onion
½ tsp garlic powder
⅓ cup tapioca starch
¼ tsp black pepper
1 tsp salt
¾ cup dark GF beer (i.e. stout or porter style)
¼ cup cream (or more stock for a vegan option)
1 batch *Plastered Pie Crust*

1. In a saucepot, combine chicken, carrots, potatoes, and peas. Add the two cups stock with enough water to cover chicken and vegetables and boil for 15 minutes. Remove from heat, drain, reserve one cup stock, and set aside.

2. In a large saucepot over medium heat, cook onions in oil or butter. Sauté until soft and translucent. Stir in garlic powder, tapioca, pepper, and salt. Add in beer and cream slowly, stirring. Simmer over medium-low heat until thick, about 5 minutes, and set aside.

3. Preheat oven to 400F. In the bottom of a pie plate, arrange chicken mixture. Pour onion and beer mix over top. Between two sheets of waxed paper, roll pie dough out about 1/8" thick. Cut to slightly larger than pie plate. Arrange pie dough over pot pie and cut an "x" in the center to let air escape.

4. Bake in oven 35 minutes. Remove from oven and let cool 10 minutes.

SOTTED CHOCOLATE CHILI (V)

This chili is rich and hearty, and you won't even miss the meat. A stout or other dark GF beer with a strong flavor is ideal, although lager makes a good substitute. Serve with *Rip-Roaring Rosemary Bread* to dip into big bowls of chili, or crumble chunks of *Cockeyed Salsa Cornbread* into it.

Serves 6

- 2 Tbsp olive oil or vegetable oil
- 1 medium-sized onion, finely diced
- 1 red bell pepper, seeded and diced
- 1 yellow or orange bell pepper, seeded and diced
- 2 cloves garlic, minced
- 1 large carrot, peeled and diced
- 1 Tbsp ground cumin
- 1 Tbsp dried oregano
- 2 Tbsp chili powder
- 1 tsp salt + more to taste
- 1 – 32 oz can diced tomatoes
- ½ cup corn kernels
- 1 – 14 oz can kidney beans
- 1 – 14 oz can black beans
- 1 – 12 oz bottle dark GF beer (stout is ideal, lager is good)
- Black pepper to taste
- 2 Tbsp cocoa powder
- Red pepper flakes or hot sauce for extra heat (optional)

Optional: sliced avocado, shredded cheese, freshly chopped cilantro, sour cream

1. In a large pot, heat oil over medium heat. Sauté onion until soft and translucent, 5-7 minutes. Add peppers, garlic, and carrot and sauté 5 minutes to soften.

2. Add cumin, oregano, chili powder, and salt. Cook 1 minute. If mix is too dry, add some juice from canned tomatoes.

3. Add tomatoes, corn, and beans. Lower heat to medium-low and simmer 15 minutes to thicken. Add beer, cocoa, and optional pepper flakes or hot sauce. Simmer 5-7 minutes. Adjust salt and pepper to taste. Serve with optional toppings.

BOOZY BEER BRINED CHICKEN

A no-fail, no-brainer for entertaining, this makes the juiciest, most tender chicken. Let it marinate overnight in the beer brine and bake it an hour before dinner. Watch the boozy, mouthwatering juices leak out and serve with sides like *Creamy Dill Asparagus, Gonzo Glazed Root Veggies,* or *Deconstructed Sorghum and Citrus Salad* for a dinner that will impress the most discriminating of guests.

Serves 6

1 – 12 oz can GF pale ale
1 cup water
2 Tbsp kosher salt
2 Tbsp brown sugar
2 bay leaves
½ lemon
2 garlic cloves
12-15 chicken thighs (or 1 small chicken)

To brush on:
1 Tbsp extra virgin olive oil
1 tsp smoked paprika
¼ tsp salt
⅛ tsp black pepper

1. In a medium-sized pot, bring beer, water, salt, sugar, bay leaves, lemon, and garlic to a simmer. Simmer 10 minutes, remove from heat and chill until room temperature. In either a 2 gallon re-sealable bag or large container with a lid, add chicken and cover with brine. Chill 8-24 hours.

2. Remove chicken and discard brine. Let chicken air dry 5 minutes. Arrange in a baking dish. Mix together olive oil, paprika, salt, and pepper and brush on chicken. Bake at 350F for 45 minutes – 1 hr, until chicken is golden brown and inside of chicken is no longer pink.

Mains

BEEN-AT-BARBADOS BATTERED FISH

Crispy on the outside and flaky on the inside, this beer battered fish will satisfy your deep fry cravings. Serve with lemon wedges and tartar sauce, and *Deconstructed Sorghum & Citrus Salad* on the side, or as show here, with *Omi's Coleslaw.*

Serves 4

2 ½ cups white rice flour, divided as per instructions
1 Tbsp baking powder
2 tsp salt
½ tsp ground black pepper
1 tsp garlic powder
1 tsp smoked paprika (optional)
1 – 12 oz bottle GF beer (pale ale or lager)
1 egg, beaten
2 – 8 oz white fish fillets (cod, haddock, sole, tilapia, etc), cut into 6" pieces
Neutral flavored oil for frying
Lemon wedges for serving (optional)

1. In a large bowl, sift together 2 cups rice flour, baking powder, salt, pepper, garlic powder, and paprika. Whisk in beer and egg until smooth.

2. On a large plate, spread out ½ cup rice flour. Rinse fish and pat dry with paper towels. Coat fish pieces with the rice flour, then dredge in the beer batter. Let excess drip off.

3. Heat enough oil to come half way up fish pieces in a large skillet, or heat oil in a deep fryer. Arrange fish in skillet or fryer, and fry 4-5 minutes on each side, until crispy and browned on the outside, and fish is white and flaky on the inside. Remove from skillet or fryer and drain on paper towels.

Mains

TIE-ONE-ON FISH TACOS

Quick and easy, these fish tacos are the next logical step for using up leftover *Been-at-Barbados Battered Fish*. If you prefer, substitute the cabbage mixture here with some leftover *Omi's Coleslaw* for a sweet and sour tangy taco.

Serves 4

>1 lb white fish (such as cod, sole, tilapia, mahi mahi) cut into strips, battered and fried according to *Been-at-Barbados Battered Fish*
>½ head green or red cabbage, shredded
>½ small red onion, thinly sliced
>¼ cup chopped fresh cilantro
>1 lime, halved
>½ Tbsp olive oil
>Salt and pepper to taste
>8 soft GF corn tortillas
>Optional: sliced avocado, prepared salsa, sour cream, guacamole, hot sauce

1. In a large bowl, toss cabbage, onion, cilantro, and juice from ½ squeezed lime. Drizzle with olive oil, toss, and add salt and pepper to taste.

2. Warm tortillas in a medium-sized frying pan over medium heat. Heating one at a time, add tortilla and warm 2-3 minutes on each side. Wrap in a clean dish towel and set aside to keep warm.

3. Lay out tortillas on a flat surface. Along the center of the tortilla, arrange a small amount of cabbage mix, top with fish and optional toppings. Wrap tortilla and serve.

BLOTTO BRATS AND KRAUT

Anyone who's been to a pub in the Midwest has probably seen bratwurst and sauerkraut on the menu. This easy beer soaked brats and kraut dish will land in your stomach with all the accompanying satisfaction of a night out at the pub. Use a mild beer with a low hops flavor, such as pale ale, to prevent too much bitterness. *Serves 4*

1 Tbsp olive oil
½ medium-sized onion, thinly sliced
1 lb fresh gluten free bratwurst style sausages
1 – 12 oz GF beer
½ Tbsp brown sugar
1 ½ tsp spicy mustard
⅛ tsp black pepper
1 lb sauerkraut, rinsed and drained
Optional: add 1 diced apple to sauce, sour cream for topping

1. Heat oil in a large skillet over medium heat. Fry onions 5-7 minutes until soft and translucent. Push onions to side and add sausages. Cook 5-7 minutes to brown.

2. Mix beer, brown sugar, mustard, and pepper. Add in optional apple if using. Pour over sausages and bring to a boil. Reduce heat to low, cover, and simmer 10 minutes.

3. Uncover, raise heat to medium, and cook until sauce is reduced and thickened, about 15 minutes. Coat sausages with sauce, then remove to a plate and keep warm. Add sauerkraut to remaining liquid in skillet and cook 5-8 minutes to absorb leftover sauce. Serve sauerkraut topped with sausages and optional sour cream.

PIE-EYED PIZZA DOUGH (V)

A soft, doughy, thick crust pizza can be hard to come by in the GF pizza world, but not when beer is added to the mix. This dough is best made with a pale ale or other citrus toned beer, and served with just about any kind of beer. Top with *Sauced Pizza Sauce* and desired toppings.

Makes 2 – 12" pizza crusts

1 cup GF beer (pale ale), heated to 110F
1 Tbsp sugar
1 packet active dry yeast
1 cup sorghum flour
1 cup brown rice flour
1 cup tapioca starch
½ tsp xanthan gum
1 tsp salt
½ tsp baking powder
Optional: ½ tsp garlic powder, ½ Tbsp dried rosemary, ¼ cup shredded cheddar cheese
3 Tbsp milk (cow, almond, rice, or soy)
1 Tbsp olive oil
1 egg (or 1 Tbsp flax meal mixed with 3 Tbsp water)

Oil two pizza pans and cover with parchment paper.

1. Mix beer, sugar, and yeast together in a small bowl. Set aside and let proof 7 minutes.

2. Sift together sorghum, rice flour, tapioca, xanthan gum, salt, baking powder, and optional garlic, herbs, and cheese (if using). Make a well in center of flours and blend in yeast mix, milk, oil, and egg. Beat until smooth. Batter will be goopy.

3. Divide dough and, using a wet spatula, spread over pans about ¼" thick. Let rise 30 minutes in a warm place, until doubled in size.

4. Pre-bake in 350F oven for 10-12 minutes, until crust is firm and lightly brown. From here, crusts can be topped with sauce (such as *Sauced Pizza Sauce*) and toppings. Bake at 375F for 10-12 minutes, until crust is browned and toppings are cooked. Alternatively, pre-baked crust (with or without toppings) can be wrapped in tin foil and frozen until needed. Remove from freezer and let defrost 15-20 before baking.

HOP-HEADED HAM

This is an incredibly easy way to bake an incredibly moist, tender, flavorful ham. A pale ale works well with ham, lending a light citrus flavor to balance the cloves and bay leaves.

1 ham shank or butt end
2 tsp brown sugar
1 tsp dry mustard
Bay leaves
Whole cloves
1-12 oz GF beer

Preheat oven to 325F.

1. In a small bowl, mix together brown sugar and dry mustard. Dribble in enough water to create a thick paste. Spread paste over ham placed in a roasting pan.

2. Cover ham entirely with bay leaves by punching cloves through the leaves, pinning them to the ham. Pour beer into the bottom of the pan (*not* over the ham). Cover ham and pan with aluminum foil. Bake in oven 20 minutes per pound of ham. Remove from oven and drain beer.

ON-A-BENDER BURGER

Burgers and beer go well side by side, and even better mixed together! Serve with a GF bun or between two slices of GF bread and topped with all the fixings. *Serves 4*

1 lb ground beef, chicken, or turkey
1 small onion, finely chopped
3 cloves garlic, minced
2 Tbsp corn meal
½ tsp salt
¼ tsp ground black pepper
⅛ cup GF beer
1 egg

Preheat an outdoor grill or large electric skillet.

1. Mix all ingredients together in a large bowl. Let rest 5 minutes to absorb beer. Form into patties and cook on grill or skillet until desired doneness, about 5 minutes on each side. A thermometer inserted inside should read about 160F / 70C.

MERRY MOON-EYED MUSSELS

Quick and easy, these steamed mussels pack a mellow, but powerful, punch. The beer sauce can be poured over the mussels, or set aside and used to dip in chunks of GF beer bread, such as *Rip-Roaring Rosemary Bread* or *Fubared Flatbread*. Serves 2-4

1 Tbsp olive oil
1 medium onion, thinly sliced
2 cloves garlic, minced
⅛ - ¼ tsp red pepper flakes (for optional heat)
1 – 1 ½ lb mussels
1 – 12oz bottle GF beer (amber or lager)
2 Tbsp butter
2 Tbsp chopped fresh parsley
Salt and pepper to taste
GF chorizo-style sausage (optional), cooked and sliced

1. In a large sauce pot, heat oil over medium heat. Sauté onion slices until soft and translucent, about 5-7 minutes. Add garlic and red pepper flakes, sauté 1 minute.

2. Rinse mussels well under cold water. Tap any opened mussels. If they do not close, discard them. Add beer and mussels to pot, lower heat to simmer and cover. Simmer 5-7 minutes, until mussels open. Any longer and mussels will become rubbery. Discard any unopened mussels.

3. Remove from heat, add butter and parsley. Remove mussels and optional sausage to a serving dish. Ladle sauce over mussels, or serve sauce on the side for dipping with *Fubared Flatbread* or *Rip-Roaring Rosemary Bread*.

Beer is a miraculously versatile ingredient, and can be slipped into all kinds of sauces, soups, and sides. It can even be broken down to its elemental parts and used in salad, as is the case in the salad shown below. In this chapter there are a couple of recipes that don't actually call for beer, but it seemed essential to include them anyway. After all, what would good pub fare be without Omi's Coleslaw?

Shown below: Deconstructed Sorghum & Citrus Salad

Chapter 4:
CAPERNOITED CONDIMENTS, SOUPS, & SIDES

Disorderly Cheddar Dip

IN THIS CHAPTER:

Disorderly Cheddar Dip	Bollixed Black Bean Soup (V)
Sauced Pizza Sauce (V)	Lager-Louted Baked Beans (V)
Giddy Gravy (V)	Off-Yer-Face Onion Rings
Muddled Meat Balls	Gonzo Glazed Root Veggies (V)
Tanked-Up Tofu Balls (V)	Deconstructed Sorghum & Citrus Salad (V)
Crocked Manhattan Clam Chowder	Creamy Dill Asparagus
Brewski Stew (V)	Omi's Coleslaw (V)

DISORDERLY CHEDDAR DIP

Perfect for game day, serve this cheddar dip warm or cold with *Fubared Flatbread,* sliced veggies, or with *Pixilated Pretzel Bites,* as shown on the previous page. Use a pale ale or lager to avoid bitterness from the hops. The use of whole milk will help prevent curdling when mixed with beer.

Makes approximately 2 cups

¾ cup whole milk, divided and chilled
1½ Tbsp white rice flour
½ cup GF beer, chilled
2 cups shredded cheddar cheese
1 tsp garlic powder
½ tsp salt
½ tsp dried onion flakes
1 tsp spicy mustard
1 tsp smoked paprika

1. Mix together ¼ cup milk with white rice flour. In a medium-sized saucepot over medium heat, add remaining milk and beer, whisking constantly. Whisk in rice flour and milk. Cook 5-7 minutes, until sauce thickens. Remove from heat and stir in remaining ingredients.

SAUCED PIZZA SAUCE (V)

Slather liberally on *Pie-Eyed Pizza Dough* for the full, booze-infused effect. *Makes 1 cup of sauce*

1 – 6 oz can tomato paste
½ cup + 1 Tbsp GF beer (pale ale, lager, or amber)
½ tsp dried oregano
½ tsp dried basil
¼ tsp ground cinnamon
1 Tbsp brown sugar
¾ tsp garlic powder
½ tsp onion flakes
Salt and pepper to taste

1. Mix all ingredients together in a medium sized bowl. Adjust salt and pepper to taste.

GIDDY GRAVY (V)

Pour over mashed potatoes, GF noodles, chicken, or any other dishes that seem to call for a quick and easy gravy. Left in the fridge overnight, this tastes even better reheated the next day, when the flavors have had time to blend. A beer without a strong hops flavor works best to avoid bitterness.

Makes approximately 3 ½ cups

2 Tbsp olive oil
1 medium onion, diced
½ Tbsp brown sugar
½ tsp salt
¼ tsp black pepper
4 oz sliced mushrooms (optional)
2 cups vegetable or chicken stock
1 – 12 oz beer (pale ale or lager)
2 bay leaves
2 Tbsp white rice flour
2 Tbsp cold water

1. In a large pot, heat olive oil over medium heat. Add grated onions, brown sugar, salt, pepper, and mushrooms (if using). Sauté 7-8 minutes, until onions are softened.

2. Add stock, beer, and bay leaves. In a small bowl, whisk together rice flour and water and add to beer mix. Bring to a boil, reduce heat and simmer for 7-10 minutes, until thickened. Remove from heat and serve warm.

MUDDLED MEAT BALLS

Serve these meatballs over rice or as a side dish. Alternatively, take them to a potluck along with plenty of toothpicks. These beer-glazed meatballs are sure to impress. You may want to serve bread on the side to dip into leftover sauce. I confess, I've been known to make the sauce alone just for dipping!

Makes 35-40 meatballs

For Meatballs:
1 lb ground beef, turkey, or chicken
1 tsp garlic powder
1 tsp dried onion flakes
1 tsp smoked paprika
½ tsp salt
4 Tbsp cornmeal or GF bread crumbs
4 Tbsp dark GF beer (ale, lager, or stout)

For Sauce:
1 Tbsp olive oil
2 cloves garlic, minced
4 Tbsp GF soy sauce (such as Bragg or Tamari)
3 Tbsp tomato paste
1 tsp smoked paprika
1 tsp onion powder
¼ - ½ tsp hot sauce (optional)
1 cup dark GF beer (ale, lager, or stout)
4 Tbsp brown sugar

Preheat oven to 400F and line a baking sheet with parchment paper.

1. To make meatballs: In a large bowl, mix together all meatball ingredients until combined. Shape into meatballs, rolling between palms. Arrange on baking sheet and bake 15 minutes, until cooked through.

2. To make the sauce: Heat oil in a medium-sized pot over medium-low heat. Add garlic and sauté 30 seconds. Add remaining sauce ingredients and simmer until thickened and reduced, about 15 minutes. Set aside.

3. In a large skillet, heat 1 Tbsp oil over medium heat. Add meatballs and cook until browned, 3-5 minutes. Add sauce and cook until sauce is thick and meatballs are glazed, 5-7 minutes.

TANKED-UP TOFU BALLS (V)

Vegans and meat eaters alike will appreciate this veggie version of *Muddled Meat Balls*. Lighter than regular meat balls, you may want to double to the recipe to ensure leftovers, as people will be inclined to eat more than usual!

Makes 30 tofu balls

For Tofu Balls:
1 package (349g / 12.3 oz) firm or extra firm organic tofu
¼ tsp sea salt
1 garlic clove
¼ tsp dried oregano
1 Tbsp ground flax mixed with 3 Tbsp warm beer or water
⅛ cup vegan, GF bread crumbs or 1 slice GF bread, toasted well and crumbled
⅛ cup fresh chopped parsley
pinch of black pepper
¼ cup white rice flour (plus ¼ - ½ cup more for dusting)
Oil for frying

For Sauce:
1 Tbsp olive oil
2 cloves garlic, minced
4 Tbsp GF soy sauce
3 Tbsp tomato paste
1 tsp smoked paprika
1 tsp onion powder
¼ - ½ tsp hot sauce (optional)
1 cup dark GF beer (ale, lager, or stout)
4 Tbsp brown sugar

1. To make tofu balls: Drain tofu by wrapping in a clean dish towel on a plate. Place a heavy plate on top and let sit 20-30 minutes to drain. In a food processor, blend all ingredients (except extra rice flour and frying oil) to make a smooth paste.

2. Add ¼ cup white rice flour to a bowl. With a spoon, scoop 1 tablespoon of tofu batter, then slide off into rice flour with the back of another spoon. Using the spoons, roll the batter through the flour to form a ball. Set aside on a plate. Repeat to finish batter, adding more rice flour as needed to coat.

3. Heat a large pan with a tablespoon or two of oil over medium heat. Add tofu balls, cover with a tight-fitting lid, and fry on one side until browned. Turn tofu balls, cover, and fry until browned.

4. To make the sauce: Heat oil in a medium sized pot over medium-low heat. Add garlic and sauté 30 seconds. Add remaining sauce ingredients and simmer until thickened and reduced, about 15 minutes. Set aside.

5. Pour sauce over tofu balls in pan and cook approximately 5-7 minutes, until sauce is thick and tofu balls are glazed.

CROCKED MANHATTAN CLAM CHOWDER

This warm and flavorful chowder can be tailored to suit your available ingredients. Substitute ¼ - ½ cup mixed seafood for one of the cans of clams, or add extra seafood and roasted peppers and top with fresh parsley. Or make this soup to use up leftover fish or seafood.

Serves 2-4

1 Tbsp olive oil
½ medium onion, finely diced
¾ cup diced carrot
1 cubed russet potato
1 clove garlic, minced
2 cups chicken or vegetable stock
1 – 15oz can diced tomatoes
1 cup GF beer (lager or ale)
2 – 6.5 oz cans clams, drained with juice reserved

½ tsp oregano
¼ tsp red pepper flakes
Salt and pepper to taste

Optional: mixed seafood (cooked scallops, shrimp, white fish or salmon), ¼ cup diced roasted red peppers, fresh parsley to garnish

1. Heat oil in a large saucepot over medium heat. Sauté onion and carrot 5-7 minutes to soften. Add potatoes, garlic, stock, and tomatoes. Bring to a boil, then reduce to simmer 20 minutes.

2. Add beer and cook 5 minutes. Add clams (and any extra seafood or roasted peppers), oregano, pepper flakes, salt and pepper and cook 2-3 minutes to heat through. Serve topped with fresh parsley if desired.

BREWSKI STEW (V)

Another warm, hearty soup that can serve as a meal all on its own, this boozy stew can be made with sausage for a meatier option, or without for a vegan one. For a rounded meal, serve with a thick slice of *Rip-Roaring Rosemary Bread* or *Cockeyed Salsa Cornbread* and a chunk of cheese on the side.

Serves 4-6

2 Tbsp olive oil
1 small onion, diced
2 cloves garlic, minced
2 bay leaves
4 cups GF chicken, beef, or vegetable stock or water
½ tsp smoked paprika
¾ tsp salt (less if using premade stock)
¼ tsp fresh ground black pepper
3 carrots, roughly chopped
2 parsnips, roughly chopped
1 russet potato, roughly chopped
1 small turnip, roughly chopped
½ cup green peas
2 Tbsp white rice
2 Tbsp red lentils
2 Tbsp white rice flour whisked into ¼ cup water
1 – 12 oz bottle beer (lager or stout)
Optional: 2 GF chorizo-style sausages, cooked and thinly sliced

1. In a large saucepot, heat oil over medium heat. Add onion and garlic and sauté until soft, about 5 minutes.

2. Add all remaining ingredients up to and excluding white rice flour and beer. Bring to a boil, reduce to simmer and cook 25 minutes, until vegetables are soft and rice is cooked.

3. Add white rice flour mixed with water, beer, and sausage (if using). Simmer 5-7 minutes to thicken. Remove from heat and serve.

BOLLIXED BLACK BEAN SOUP (V)

This black bean soup is satisfying, whether you make it with or without sausage. Double the recipe for leftovers, or freeze some for later. Serve with *Cock-Eyed Salsa Cornbread, Fubared Flatbread,* or *Rip-Roaring Rosemary Bread*, or GF tortilla chips for dipping.

Serves 4

2 – 15 oz cans black beans
1 tablespoon olive oil
1 small onion, minced
2 carrots, chopped
2 cloves garlic, minced
1 Tbsp chili powder
½ Tbsp ground cumin
½ tsp salt
¼ tsp black pepper
1 cup vegetable stock
1 – 14.5 oz can crushed tomatoes
1 cup GF beer (lager, stout, ale)
1 large GF chorizo-style sausage, cooked and chopped (optional)
Optional toppings: chopped fresh cilantro, hot sauce, shredded cheddar cheese, yogurt, sour cream, nutritional yeast

1. In a food processor, roughly purée the black beans, leaving some beans still chunky. Set aside.

2. In a large saucepot, heat oil over medium heat. Add onion and sauté 5-7 minutes, until soft. Add carrots and garlic. Sauté 1 minute. Add chili powder, cumin, salt, pepper, stock, tomatoes, and puréed beans. Simmer 20 minutes, until thickened.

3. Add in beer and chorizo sausage (if using). Cook 5-7 minutes, until thickened. Adjust salt and pepper to taste and serve topped with optional toppings.

Soups, Salads & Sides

LAGER-LOUTED BAKED BEANS (V)

Nothing says comfort food like baked beans. This classic recipe has been given an update by baking the beans in a boozy tomato sauce and whether you make it vegan or loaded with bacon and ham, it makes a great side dish. For a satisfying lunch, pair it with a slice of *Cockeyed Salsa Cornbread, Rip-Roaring Rosemary Bread,* or *Bacchic Biscuits.*

Serves 8

>2 cups dry white beans (such as Navy, Great Northern, or cannellini beans)*
>2 bay leaves
>½ medium-sized onion, finely diced
>3 Tbsp molasses or maple syrup
>1 ½ tsp salt
>¼ tsp ground black pepper
>¼ tsp dry mustard
>1 tsp smoked paprika
>¼ cup brown sugar
>6 Tbsp ketchup
>1 – 12 oz GF beer (lager or pale ale)
>Optional: 1 lb bacon or cubed ham hock

1. Soak beans in water overnight, or 8-10 hours. Drain and rinse. In a large pot, cover with water, add bay leaves, and bring to a boil. Reduce to simmer and cover. Simmer 45 minutes – 1 hr, until soft. Drain, mix with onion, and layer with optional bacon or ham in an oven-safe casserole dish.

2. In a small saucepan, mix molasses, salt, pepper, mustard, paprika, sugar, ketchup, and beer. Heat over medium heat and whisk until all ingredients are dissolved. Pour over beans and cover with a tight-fitting lid or aluminum foil.

3. Bake in 350F oven for 1 ½ -2 hours. Half-way through, baste beans and remove lid. Continue cooking until beans are soft and beer sauce is reduced. Remove from oven and let cool slightly before serving.

* To skip the soaking and cooking process, use approximately 3-15oz cans of white beans.

OFF-YER-FACE ONION RINGS

Beer and onion rings go together like peas in a pod. Serve as an appetizer, or with a pub-style dish like *Blotto Brats and Kraut*.

Serves 2-4

- 2 ½ cups white rice flour, divided as per instructions
- 1 Tbsp baking powder
- 2 tsp salt
- ½ tsp ground black pepper
- 1 tsp garlic powder
- 1 tsp smoked paprika (optional)
- 1 – 12 oz bottle GF beer (pale ale or lager)
- 1 egg, beaten
- 2 sweet onions, sliced in rounds
- Oil for frying

1. In a large bowl, sift together 2 cups rice flour, baking powder, salt, pepper, garlic powder, and paprika. Whisk in beer and egg until mixture is smooth.

2. In a large freezer bag, add ½ cup rice flour. Add onion slices to the bag, seal, and shake to coat slices with flour. Dip onions slices in beer batter to coat.

3. Heat approximately ½" oil in a large pan. Arrange onion rings in skillet and fry 4-5 minutes on each side, until crispy and browned on the outside. Remove from fryer and drain on paper towels.

GONZO GLAZED ROOT VEGGIES (V)

Warm with just a touch of sweetness, beer gives roasted root vegetables a rich fall flavor. Serve these veggies alongside *Boozy Beer Brined Chicken, Merry Moon-Eyed Mussels,* or *Tie-One-On Fish Tacos* for a complete dinner, or with *Deconstructed Sorghum and Citrus Salad* for a satisfying lunch. *Serves 4*

- 2 Tbsp butter or olive oil
- 4 cups mixed seasonal root vegetables (carrots, turnips, parsnips, potatoes, etc), peeled and chopped into ½" chunks
- ½ cup chicken or vegetable stock
- ¾ cup GF beer (lager or ale)
- 2 Tbsp honey or brown sugar
- 1 Tbsp fresh chopped rosemary
- Salt and pepper to taste

1. In large pot over medium heat, melt butter, or heat oil. Add vegetables and cook 5 minutes to soften.

2. Add stock and beer. Simmer 10-15 minutes to reduce and soften vegetables. Add remaining ingredients, adjusting salt and pepper to taste. Remove from heat and serve.

DECONSTRUCTED SORGHUM & CITRUS SALAD (V)

Sorghum, clover honey, and citrus are all used for brewing beer. Here those ingredients have been deconstructed to serve as the inspiration for a sweet, citrusy side salad. Sorghum syrup is available in the health section of many grocery stores. It is a bit like molasses, and can be used to sweeten in place of honey or molasses, or slathered over warm slices of *Rip-Roaring Rosemary Bread*. Clover flowers add a touch of bitterness, like the hops used in the brewing process, and can be found growing in lawns and gardens in the summer time. *Serves 4*

<u>Citrus Salad Dressing</u>
1 Tbsp spicy mustard
2 Tbsp concentrated orange juice
1 Tbsp olive oil
2 tsp sorghum syrup
1 Tbsp red wine vinegar
2 Tbsp water

<u>Salad Ingredients</u>
4 cups loosely packed mixed greens or spinach
1 ½ cups baby beets, or 2 large beets
¼ cup cashews
2 Tbsp dried cranberries
½ cup fresh clover flowers (optional)
¼ cup feta cheese (optional)

1. In a microwave-safe container, mix together all ingredients for salad dressing. Heat in a microwave for 15 seconds to soften sorghum syrup. Stir to blend.

2. Bake beets in an oven-safe dish at 425F for 30 minutes – 1 hr, until a knife can be inserted easily. Remove and cool until easy to handle. Peel and slice.

3. Toss all salad ingredients together and drizzle with dressing.

Soups, Salads & Sides

CREAMY DILL ASPARAGUS

Yogurt and dill with asparagus makes a light side dish to balance the heavier flavors of beer infused entrées. Serve alongside *Boozy Beer Brined Chicken, Muddle Meat Balls, Tanked-Up Tofu Balls, Merry Moon-Eyed Mussels,* or *Poor Man's Pierogi*.

Serves 4

1 lb fresh asparagus
1 clove garlic, minced
1 Tbsp lemon juice
1 cup plain yogurt
½ tsp salt
⅛ tsp pepper
1 Tbsp freshly minced dill

1. Mix together garlic, lemon, yogurt, salt, pepper, and dill. Chill 1 hour before use to let flavors blend.

2. In a steaming basket, steam asparagus 5-7 minutes, until softened. Serve topped with dill and yogurt sauce.

OMI'S COLESLAW (V)

This sweet and sour coleslaw is modelled after the coleslaw my German Omi used to serve alongside bratwurst, and battered, fried fish, like *Been-at-Barbados Battered Fish*. One could easily substitute the cabbage filling in *Tie-One-On Fish Tacos* with this tangy coleslaw.

Serves 6

1 medium-sized head cabbage, shredded
1 cup grated carrot
½ red onion, diced
¼ cup sugar
½ cup white vinegar
2 Tbsp olive oil
¼ tsp salt

1. In a large bowl, toss together all ingredients. Let chill 1-2 hours before serving for flavors to blend.

Beer goes great with desserts, enhancing the lush, deep flavor of chocolate and baked goods. Full-bodied stouts and lagers work particularly well in the truffles, cakes, and doughnuts in this chapter.

Shown below: Trashed Truffles

Chapter 5:
DIONYSIAN DESSERTS

Four-to-the-Floor Chocolate Icing

IN THIS CHAPTER:

Clobbered Chocolate Applesauce Cake (V)

Bacchanalian Brownies

Borracho Mexican Chocolate Cupcakes with Kahlua Frosting

Legless Light Chocolate Cupcakes (V)

A Cup-Too-Much Pie Crust (V)

Furshnickered Apple Fritters (V)

Trashed Truffles

Mini Dipso Doughnuts (V)

Peely-Wally Pudding (V)

Got-Your-Woobly-Boots-On Glaze (V)

Jolly Chocolate Glaze (V)

Four-to-the-Floor Chocolate Icing (V)

CLOBBERED CHOCOLATE APPLESAUCE CAKE (V)

This chocolate cake is a light, moist, healthy take on the typical sugar and butter laden chocolate beer cake. A darker, malty beer, such as a stout, will provide a deeper flavor, while a citrus pale ale will allow the gentle applesauce flavor to come through.

Makes 1-6 cup Bundt pan

¼ cup soft butter (or olive oil or coconut oil)
2 eggs (or 2 Tbsp flax meal mixed with 6 Tbsp water)
½ cup brown sugar
¾ cup dark GF beer, at room temp
⅓ cup applesauce
1 Tbsp apple cider vinegar
1 tsp vanilla extract

1 cup sorghum flour
¼ cup millet flour
¼ cup cocoa
¾ cup tapioca starch
2 tsp baking powder
1 tsp baking soda
1 ½ tsp xanthan gum
¾ cup chocolate chips or cacao nibs

Preheat oven to 350F and grease a 6 cup Bundt pan.

1. Whisk together butter, eggs, and sugar in a large bowl until fluffy. Blend in beer, applesauce, cider vinegar, and vanilla.

2. In a medium-sized bowl, sift together all dry ingredients except chocolate chips. Fold dry ingredients into beer mix and blend until smooth. Fold in chocolate chips. Pour into Bundt pan and smooth the top with a wet spatula.

3. Bake for 35-40 minutes, until a toothpick inserted in the center comes out clean. Tap Bundt pan over a cooling rack to pop out cake and let cool 15 minutes to set before cutting. Serve drizzled with *Kahlua Frosting, Got-Your-Woobly-Boots-On Glaze,* or *Jolly Chocolate Glaze.*

BACCHANALIAN BROWNIES

Rich and moist, these beer brownies are the perfect ending to a boozy dinner.

Makes one 8x8" baking dish

½ cup dark GF beer
6 Tbsp cocoa powder
6 Tbsp butter
2 eggs
¾ cup brown sugar
1 tsp vanilla
½ cup sorghum or brown rice flour
¼ cup tapioca starch
¼ tsp xanthan gum
½ tsp salt
½ tsp baking powder
Optional: ½ cup chocolate chips

Preheat oven to 350F and grease an 8x8" baking dish.

1. In a heavy saucepan, heat beer over medium-low heat. Simmer until thickened, about 10 minutes. Whisk in butter and cocoa. Remove from heat and cool.

2. Whisk together eggs, sugar, and vanilla until smooth. Whisk beer mixture into egg mix.

3. Sift together remaining dry ingredients. Fold dry ingredients into beer mixture and beat until smooth. Fold in chocolate chips, if using.

4. Pour into baking dish and bake 18-20 minutes, until a toothpick inserted in the center comes out clean. Remove from oven and cool 15 minutes to set before slicing into squares.

Desserts

BORRACHO MEXICAN CHOCOLATE CUPCAKES
WITH KAHLUA FROSTING

Sweet, spicy, moist, and unusual, these cupcakes would make a fantastic end to a dinner of *Sotted Chocolate Chili* and *Cockeyed Salsa Cornbread*.

Makes approximately 18 cupcakes

1 cup unsalted butter	1 tsp xanthan gum
½ cup cocoa powder	1 tsp baking soda
¼ cup brewed coffee	1 tsp cinnamon
½ cup dark GF beer	¾ tsp chili powder
1½ cup sugar	¼ tsp salt
2 eggs	
½ cup milk	Kahlua Frosting
1 ½ tsp vanilla	1 Tbsp Kahlua
	½ Tbsp soft butter
1¼ cup sorghum flour	1 cup icing sugar + extra as needed
¾ cup tapioca starch	

Heat oven to 350F and grease two muffin tins or line with cupcake liners.

1. Melt butter in a heavy saucepan over low heat. Whisk in cocoa, coffee, and beer until smooth. Remove from heat and separately whisk in sugar, eggs, milk, and vanilla.

2. Sift together dry ingredients then mix into butter and beer mixture until just combined. Scoop into muffin tins ¾ full. Bake approximately 20 minutes, until a toothpick inserted in the muffins comes out clean. Cool in pan 20 minutes, until set. Top with *Kahlua Frosting, Four-to-the-Floor Chocolate Icing, Got-Your-Woobly-Boots-On Glaze,* or *Jolly Chocolate Glaze*.

3. **To make Kahlua Frosting:** Mix Kahlua, butter, and sugar until smooth, adding icing sugar as needed to create a stiff mixture.

Desserts

Legless Light Chocolate Cupcakes with Four-to-the-Floor Chocolate icing

LEGLESS LIGHT CHOCOLATE CUPCAKES (V)

These chocolate cupcakes whisk up quickly but lose nothing in the flavor department. Stouts, ales, and lagers work well in these. Make sure the beer and milk are both cold when whisked together to prevent curdling.

Makes approximately 12 cupcakes

¾ cup cold dark GF beer
¼ cup milk (cow, almond, rice, or soy milk)
½ cup brown sugar
⅓ cup oil (or 3 Tbsp applesauce and 2 ½ Tbsp oil)
1 tsp vanilla extract

¾ cup sorghum flour
¼ cup tapioca starch
¾ tsp xanthan gum
⅓ cup cocoa powder
½ Tbsp baking powder
½ tsp baking soda
¼ tsp salt

Preheat oven to 350F and grease a muffin tin or line with cupcake liners.

1. Whisk cold beer and milk in a large bowl, combining slowly. Whisk in sugar, oil, and vanilla and beat until foamy. Set aside.

2. In a medium-sized bowl, sift together dry ingredients. Add ½ dry ingredients to wet mix and beat in. Add remaining ½ mix and beat until smooth. Fill cupcake liners ¾ full. Bake 15-20 minutes until a toothpick inserted in the center comes out clean. Let cool 15 minutes to set. Top with *Kahlua Frosting, Four-to-the-Floor Chocolate Icing, Got-Your-Woobly-Boots-On Glaze,* or *Jolly Chocolate Glaze.*

A CUP-TOO-MUCH PIE CRUST (V)

An easy, versatile pie crust that can be used with *Tipsy Pot Pie*, or bake and fill with a fresh batch of *Peely-Wally Pudding* and chill to set for a chocolate pudding pie.

Males 1 – 9" pie crust

¾ cup sorghum flour
½ c tapioca starch
¼ c sweet rice flour
8 Tbsp butter, or dairy free alternative, chilled and chopped into chunks
¼ c cold GF beer (pale ale works well)
Ice water as needed

1. In a food processor, add sorghum, tapioca, and sweet rice flour. Pulse to blend. Add butter and pulse just until blended and dough is crumbly. Alternatively, use a large bowl, sift dry ingredients, then cut in butter using a pastry cutter or two knives.

2. Slowly add the beer and continue pulsing until the dough forms a ball. Add ice water by the tablespoon as needed and continue pulsing until ball is formed.

3. Turn the ball of dough onto a sheet of plastic wrap or waxed paper, wrap, and chill for about 10 minutes.

4. To use dough, remove from fridge. Roll out dough in between two sheets of waxed paper about ⅛" thick. Cut to slightly larger than a pie plate.

To pre-bake crust: In a pie plate with dough cut to size, prick dough with a fork to prevent bubbling, and bake crust 10 minutes at 350F, until lightly browned.

FURSHNICKERED APPLE FRITTERS (V)

Beer batter makes these fritters crispier on the outside than typical fritters, but that only means that it's an even more appealing contrast to the sweet, soft apple goodness on the inside. Using less oil in the pan also makes for a slightly less greasy (and healthier!) fritter. Dip the fritters in the cinnamon sugar dusting, or in *Got-Your-Woobly-Boots-On Glaze*. These never last long enough for me to photograph so if you're having guests over, be sure to double to recipe!

Serves 4

½ cup white rice flour
¼ cup tapioca starch
1 ½ tsp baking powder
¼ cup white sugar
¾ tsp salt
1 tsp cinnamon
⅓ cup GF beer (pale ale or lager)
1 egg (or 1 Tbsp flax meal mixed with 3 Tbsp water)
1 tsp vanilla extract
1 cup chopped crisp apple
Oil for frying

<u>Cinnamon Sugar Dusting</u>
¼ cup white sugar
½ tsp cinnamon

1. Sift together rice flour, tapioca, baking powder, sugar, salt, and cinnamon. Whisk in beer, egg, and vanilla. Fold in apple chunks.

2. Heat approximately ¼" oil in a large skillet over medium to medium-low heat. Drop a small sample of batter into the pan to check the heat. If the batter sizzles, it's hot enough. If it burns, it is too hot. Drop spoonfuls of batter into the oil. Fry until golden brown on one side, then flip and fry on the other. Drain on a plate covered in paper towels. Repeat with remaining batter, adding oil as needed.

3. To make the cinnamon sugar dusting, mix sugar and cinnamon in a small bowl. Dip the drained fritters in the mix, dusting both sides. Alternatively, dip into a batch of *Got-Your-Woobly-Boots-On Glaze*.

TRASHED TRUFFLES

Rich, not-too-sweet, and dark, these truffles will satisfy any chocolate craving. Top with a variety of optional toppings, or a mix of toppings, or add orange zest along with the chopped chocolate for a delicious citrus and beer flavor.

Makes approximately 50 truffles

8 oz good quality dark chocolate (60% cocoa or more), chopped
½ cup dark GF beer (lager, ale, or stout)
½ cup heavy cream

Optional coatings: good quality melted chocolate, coarse sea salt, cocoa powder, crushed nuts, coconut flakes, chili powder, ground espresso

1. In a heavy bottomed pot over medium heat, whisk beer and cream until frothy and almost boiling. *Do not* bring to a boil and scald milk. Pour over chopped chocolate in a medium-sized bowl. Chill about 2 hours.

2. Using a small spoon or melon baller, scoop out chocolate and roll into a ball. Dip in optional coatings and chill on a plate 20 minutes – 1 hr before serving.

MINI DIPSO DOUGHNUTS (V)

Remarkably simple, these bite-sized doughnuts are delicious. Nobody needs to know they're healthier than their glutinous, fried counterparts. Glaze and freeze these for a quick dessert. No need to defrost or reheat, they're just as good frozen as they are at room temp!

Makes 24-30 doughnuts

½ cup brown rice flour
¼ cup tapioca starch
¼ cup sweet rice flour
¼ cup sugar
1 tsp baking powder
¼ tsp baking soda
½ tsp xanthan gum
¼ tsp salt
½ cup GF beer at room temp (pale ale or lager)
2 Tbsp olive oil
3 Tbsp applesauce (or more oil or softened butter)
½ tsp vanilla extract

Preheat oven to 350F and lightly oil a mini doughnut pan.

1. In a large bowl, sift together brown rice flour, tapioca, sweet rice flour, sugar, baking powder, baking soda, xanthan, and salt.

2. Whisk together beer, oil, applesauce, and vanilla. Gradually mix wet ingredients into flour mix until smooth.

3. Fill a piping bag, or re-sealable plastic bag with a hole cut out of one corner, with batter and pipe into doughnut pan ¾ full. Bake for 10 minutes, until springy to the touch, and cool on a rack. Glaze with *Got-Your-Wobbly-Boots-On Glaze* or *Jolly Chocolate Glaze*.

Desserts

PEELY-WALLY PUDDING (V)

This rich, dark chocolate pudding is so quick and easy to make. Scoop into individual serving cups, or pour over a pre-baked crust of *A Cup-Too-Much Pie Crust*.

Serves 6

1 ½ Tbsp cocoa
2 Tbsp corn starch or tapioca starch
¼ tsp salt
2 Tbsp sugar (or more for added sweetness)
¾ cup cold dark beer (lager or stout)
¼ cup cold heavy cream (coconut milk or rice milk)
2 oz dark chocolate, chopped
½ tsp vanilla

1. In a microwave safe bowl, sift cocoa, starch, salt, and sugar. Slowly whisk in beer and cream. If both cream and beer are cold there is less likelihood of curdling. Add in chopped chocolate.

2. Microwave on high 2 minutes. Stir, then cook in 30 second increments, stirring and heating until chocolate is melted and pudding becomes thick and shiny. Add in vanilla and stir.

3. Divide pudding into serving cups and chill until cool and thick.

GOT-YOUR-WOOBLY-BOOTS-ON GLAZE (V)

The simplest glaze for *Furshnickered Apple Fritters*, *Mini-Dipso Doughnuts*, *Legless Light Chocolate Cupcakes*, or *Clobbered Chocolate Applesauce Cake*. Pale ale provides a citrus glaze flavor, while lagers, ales, and stouts make for a slightly stronger beer flavored glaze.

Makes ½ cup glaze

1 Tbsp GF beer
½ cup icing sugar

1. In a small bowl, whisk together ingredients. Adjust beer and icing sugar as needed to create a smooth glaze.

JOLLY CHOCOLATE GLAZE (V)

Another quick and easy topping, this chocolate glaze is great on *Mini-Dipso Doughnuts, Legless Light Chocolate Cupcakes,* or *Clobbered Chocolate Applesauce Cake.*

Makes ½ cup glaze

1 Tbsp dark GF beer
½ cup icing sugar
1 Tbsp cocoa powder
1 Tbsp butter, softened (or dairy-free substitute)
¼ tsp vanilla extract

1. In a small bowl, whisk all ingredients together. Adjust beer and icing sugar as needed to create a smooth glaze.

FOUR-TO-THE-FLOOR CHOCOLATE ICING (V)

The perfect icing for *Borracho Mexican Chocolate Cupcakes, Legless Light Chocolate Cupcakes,* or *Clobbered Applesauce Cake,* this icing has a deep, chocolate flavor that isn't too sweet.

Makes enough to ice 12 cupcakes or 1 cake

2 ⅔ cups icing sugar
½ cup cocoa powder
6 Tbsp softened butter (or dairy free substitute)
1 Tbsp milk (cow, rice, soy, almond, etc.)
3 Tbsp dark GF beer
¾ tsp vanilla extract

1. In a medium-sized bowl, sift together icing sugar and cocoa powder.

2. In a large bowl, cream butter until smooth. Gradually beat in ½ the sugar mix. Blend in milk, beer, and vanilla. Add remaining sugar mix and beat until light and smooth. Add more milk or icing sugar if needed to adjust consistency. Apply with a piping bag or knife to cupcakes and cake.

THANK YOU FOR CHOOSING COOKING AND BAKING WITH GLUTEN FREE BEER

If you enjoyed this book, please consider writing a review on Amazon, Goodreads.com, or other locations.

Your reviews mean a lot to me, and help others to find these cookbooks so they can benefit from them also.

For gluten free beer reviews, resources, free recipes, articles, and more information on going gluten free or living with food allergies, follow me, Danielle S. LeBlanc and my blog
www.PoorandGlutenFree.blogspot.com.

Find Danielle on Google + under:
Poor and Gluten Free

Follow Poor and Gluten Free on Facebook at:
Poor and Gluten Free (Gluten Free on a Budget)

Find recipes and DIY projects on Pinterest at:
http://www.pinterest.com/glutenfreecheap/

For updates on other publications from La Venta West, Inc check out
www.LaVentaWestPublishers.blogpost.com

MORE FROM DANIELLE S. LEBLANC

Recipes for Unusual Gluten Free Pasta: Pierogis, Dumplings, Desserts and More!

Pasta isn't just about spaghetti. It's about ravioli, won tons, steamed dumpling buns, gnocchi, and other delicious dishes that are often out of reach for those with gluten intolerance or celiac disease. *Recipes for Unusual Gluten Free Pasta* makes it possible for people to enjoy gluten-free pasta at its best.

From traditional favorites like fresh fettuccine and pierogi to lesser-known delights such as Turkish piruhi and Polish kopytka, you'll find a wide variety of interesting and unusual pasta from around the globe, brought straight to your kitchen in simple to follow recipes. As a bonus, most recipes have been given a healthy update and offer vegan, dairy-free, and egg-free options.

Discover over 60 unusual recipes and combinations such as:

* Ravioli Nudi
* Steamed Dumpling Buns (Bao)
* Tri Colored Tortellini
* Hand-cut Orzo
* Chocolate Ganache filled Chocolate Ravioli Dough

Move beyond store-bought brown rice pasta and start making your own fresh gluten-free pasta today!

Living with Oral Allergy Syndrome: A Gluten and Meat-Free Cookbook for Soy, Wheat, Fresh Fruit and Vegetable Allergies

By Danielle S. LeBlanc
With a Foreword from Dr. Rod LeBlanc, DTCM

If your lips, mouth or tongue have ever tingled after eating fresh fruits or vegetables, if wheat makes you wheeze, if soy makes you sick, or if nuts knock you out, there's a good chance you have oral allergy syndrome, a hay-fever related food allergy. Oral allergy syndrome, also known as pollen food allergy syndrome or food pollen allergy, occurs when people react to foods that are related to certain pollens. For example, if you're allergic to birch pollen, you may notice your lips tingle when you eat a fresh apple, peach or almonds. If you're allergic to grass, ragweed or latex, you might find that kiwis, bananas or tomatoes give you hives or belly aches.

Oral allergy syndrome is the leading cause of food allergies, with 50-90% of people with hay fever suffering from related food allergies. However, it is little understood and often goes unrecognized, unreported and undiagnosed. Those with it often feel frustrated by the lack of information about it, and may be confused about what to eat. If any of this applies to you, you'll want to read this book, the most comprehensive resource on oral allergy syndrome to date.

This book will help you to:

* Understand what OAS is and learn its possible origins and treatments
* Manage hay fever and food allergies
* Avoid foods with hidden allergens
* Deal with eating out and cooking at home
* Find nutritious snacks and basic meal suggestions
* Cook around your restrictions and maintain a balanced diet
* Take control of your health and overall wellbeing

And it includes over 60 healthy recipes for oral allergy syndrome free of gluten, meat, wheat, soy, and OAS related nuts, most of which are also dairy-free or with dairy-free options!

INDEX

A

Apple Fritters, 72
Asparagus, with Creamy Dill Sauce, 62

B

Battered Fish, 40
Beans
    Baked in Beer, 58
    Black Bean Soup, 56
Beer Brined Chicken, 38
Beer Glaze, 76
Biscuits, 22
Black Bean Soup, 56
Brats and Kraut, 43
Burgers, 45

C

Cheddar Dip, 49
Chicken
    Beer-Brined, 38
    Pot Pie, 36
Chocolate
    Brownies, 66
    Chocolate Applesauce Cake, 65
    Chocolate Glaze, 77
    Chocolate Icing, 77
    Light Chocolate Cupcakes, 70
    Mexican Chocolate Cupcakes, 68
    Pudding, 76
    Truffles, 73
Chocolate Chili, 37
Cinnamon Rolls, 26
Clam Chowder, 54
Coleslaw, Omi's, 62
Cornbread, with Salsa, 28
Crepes, Sweet Potato, 24

D

Doughnuts, 74

F

Fish
    Beer Battered & Fried, 40
    Tacos, 42
Flatbread, 21
French Toast, 20

G

Gravy, 50

H

Ham, Cooked in Beer, 45

M

Meat Balls, 51
Mussels, Steamed in beer, 46

O

Onion Rings, 59

P

Pie Crust, 71
Pizza Dough, 44
Pizza Sauce, 49
Poor Man's Pierogi, 35
Pot Pie, 36
Pretzel Bites, 30

R

Root Veggies, Glazed, 59
Rosemary Bread, 32

S

Salad, Sorghum & Citrus, 60

Scones, Blueberry, 19
Stew, 55

T

Tofu Balls, 53
Truffles, 73

www.ingramcontent.com/pod-product-compliance
Lightning Source LLC
Chambersburg PA
CBHW061930290426
44113CB00024B/2860